CROSS SECTIONS

A POETRY COLLECTION

BY MATT SCHUR

First paperback edition May 2021

Book and cover design by pixelstudio

ISBN 978-0-578-90372-9 (paperback)
ISBN 978-0-578-90371-2 (ebook)

www.authormattschur.wordpress.com

To my wife Karin. For over 20 years, you've been the poetry in my life. I'm so grateful for you, for your love and support, and for the life we've built together. I will be here—no matter what.

And to Tyler and Brianna. May you always walk in the way of Jesus: loving your neighbor, welcoming the stranger, standing up for the marginalized, speaking truth to power, and even overturning a table or two if the situation calls for it (just not the one in our kitchen, please).

TABLE OF CONTENTS

SECTION 1: THE CROSS IN OUR LIVES

GALATIANS 6:2

Come. Let us sit.
Let us just be for a moment.
Or for many moments.
Let my presence be a safe space,
a soft place for you to land.
You say you're falling,
that the once solid ground beneath you
                silently cracked
                slowly crumbled away
                and left you plunging into the abyss.
The thing of it was, you say,
you could watch it happening
like a movie
or a dream—
that one dream where your feet are stuck,
which (you heard somewhere)
invades the brain when someone feels stuck
and maybe you were, you ponder out loud
but
now
you're
plummeting
and you would give anything to be stuck again
back then at least the surroundings were familiar
when you were slow dancing with the devil you know.

Sometimes the most devastating earthquakes
are the little ones
the ones you barely notice at first
the ones that you're sure you can handle
looking down you see solid ground
no cracks
no crumbling.
You can't even feel that your feet are stuck.
You've got this handled so
there's no emergency
        no fight or flight
no need to even move
because you're safe.

Except
you're not.

Beneath the fresh green grass
mowed so neatly
trimmed with care
a deep cavern opens out of sight—
a dark pit gradually weakening the ground
preparing to devour you
while you obliviously stand
until the slow-motion uncontrolled descent begins
and
        you
                fall.

You tell me all of this, adding a bitter irony:
the earthquake that finally finished
breaking the earth open beneath you,

sending you hurtling toward oblivion...
that one was hardly anything.
Barely a blip on your personal seismograph.

I too have felt the ground give way beneath me.
I too have experienced that hideous downward death spiral,
wondering if this hole is limitless
or worse, what awaits at the bottom.
Will I be dashed against the rocks,
a crushed, lifeless body?
Could survival somehow be worse?
Could I spend eternity alone, broken, bleeding?
Yes, I have felt all those things.

Our feet may have rested on different terrain
the ground rumbling beneath us may have shaken

with a different frequency
or a different intensity

        but the falling? Yes.
        the fear? Yes.
        the helplessness? Yes.
        the pit? Yes.

So come here. Let us sit.
Let us just be for a moment.
Or for many moments.
Let my presence be a safe space
a soft place for you to land.
You say you're falling
And I've fallen too.
But I survived the landing.

And I found a way out.
I may not have exact directions
or definitive answers,
precisely which way to climb
or where the rocks in your particular cavern
have the best handholds and footholds,
but I have experience in falling, and landing, and climbing out,
and I do know this much:
there is always reason for hope.
Always.
And there is always a way back to the surface.
Always.

When the time has come for us to no longer sit
let us search together
let us climb together
let me support you
as together
we rise toward the sunlight.
You are not alone.

DEPRESSIVE FAITH

Jesus loves me this I know
no he doesn't
       you worthless pile of shit
       you screwup
       you waste of potential
       you burden to your friends
            to your family
            to every person in your past
            present
            and time yet to come
everyone who ever believed in you
            who had faith in you
who actually thought you were worth something.

Look at you
they all hate you even more than you hate yourself
and that's what you deserve
       not their love but their scorn
       not their support but their rejection
       not their trust but their doubt
now this, this is something I know:
Jesus does not love you
and neither does anybody else.

I remember those conversations with myself
       back before the venlafaxine
       back before the bupropion

back before the therapy
back when "God has a plan for you"
was a threat.
If God was counting on me
to live up to some sort of plan
that meant I could screw it up
like I screwed everything else up
    (and let's be honest
    it was only a matter of time).
Way to go, loser.
Jesus doesn't love you.

If my heart had arrhythmia
if my lungs had asthma
if my pancreas didn't produce insulin
if my body was allergic to wheat gluten
nobody would question my faith
nobody would call me a bad Christian if I had
    a blood disease
    a gastro-intestinal disorder
    a hearing issue.

But since it's my brain
since it's out of whack levels of serotonin
    instead of insulin
since it's malfunctioning synapses
    or receptors
instead of heart valves
    or clotting agents
they tell me I have a defective faith
they tell me I'm sinning against God
they tell me I'm a hypocrite.

My therapist once told me that depression is a liar.
"Matt," she said
"When you are your best self," she said
"What is one thing you know to be true?
One thing about yourself that is
                              always
                              unquestionably
                              undoubtedly
                              true?"

        "I am a baptized
        and beloved
        child of God."

When the venlafaxine and the bupropion
are doing their job with my serotonin
                              and synapses
I understand completely
unquestioningly
catechetically
that this is most certainly true.

When the depression is lying
and the synapses are misfiring
if the message I'm getting
contradicts the truth
        it's a lie.
Even if it feels true
        it's a lie.
Even if it seems true with every fiber of my being
        it's a lie.

I still have days
my brain is faithless
        though I am not
and my brain is a hypocrite
        though I am not
and my brain is a bad Christian
        though I am not

My best self knows better
        (even if it's hidden for a time)
My healthy brain knows better
        (even if it's temporarily unhealthy)
I know better, and I am more than the sum
of my synapses and serotonin.
Jesus loves me.
This I know.

A Mother's Prayer

Dedicated to my mother, Sharon.

"Our Father who art in heaven"
A late April early morning
in an Air Force hospital delivery room.
A labored Amen at the conclusion of a nine-month prayer
spoken with hopes and plans
but punctuated with tears and "I know you didn't
                          hope or plan
for this, but you need a c-section."

"Hallowed be thy name."
I'm told you weren't awake when I was born.
I'm told you weren't awake when your new baby's seizures began
or when they hurriedly baptized him in the delivery room sink
before speeding him an hour away by ambulance,
sirens screaming, preparing a path to
the big city children's hospital
where specialists and salvation awaited.

"Thy kingdom come"
I'm told you were awake
when the pronouncement came that Matthew
likely had brain damage
resulting from the trauma of his birth.
He would probably walk at some point, they said.
Even if with the help of braces, they said.
But, they said, he most likely would never learn to read.

But then, two brief years later, when your son
(who was already walking)
began to read?
You were awake then, too.

"Thy will be done"
I'm told the sacrifices of a military spouse can be difficult.
Raising two kids while attending nursing school—a Herculean labor.
As one woman, you took the job of
                              two parents
                              every third week
when the Air Force made the alert facility or the seat of a B-52
Dad's temporary Cold War home
safeguarding us all from Soviet missiles.

"On earth as it is in heaven."
One day you talked your first-grade son into piano lessons.
"Wouldn't you like to play like I do?" you asked.
Of course I would.
I had looked on in awe as
your virtuoso fingers glided effortlessly across the keyboard,
creating angelic melodies—of course I wanted to emulate that
except
soon it was no longer easy
and I no longer wanted to emulate that
and I asked to quit

"Give us this day our daily bread"
I kept asking as you kept bringing me to lessons
I would throw tantrums as you kept bringing me to lessons
I would hide my piano books as you kept bringing me to lessons
I would refuse to practice as you kept bringing me to lessons

"And forgive us our trespasses"
And now that tantrum throwing book hiding practice refusing kid
is teaching his own child—your granddaughter--how to play the piano
in-between playing for church services and other gigs.
You didn't let me give up
just as you never gave up in school
(class valedictorian)
or in nursing school
(class valedictorian)

"As we forgive those who trespass against us."
You still never gave up when you began to lose track of conversations
      and couldn't figure out email anymore
      and the notes on the page disappeared
                before your fingers could convert them to
piano melodies
      and the words in your books no longer made sense
      and your brain kept telling you that your newborn grandson
didn't like you
      and you emotionally beat yourself up knowing that you
should know
                              how to
write a check
                but the numbers no longer computed
        even though it used to be a simple task
      and when the words started to disappear
      and when the incontinence started to appear

"And lead us not into temptation"
      and when you no longer knew who your grandchildren were
        who your children were
        who your husband was
        who you were

"But deliver us from evil"
There was a time some years ago when you could no longer talk
all that much
and your eyes stared vacantly
   not entirely present
   not entirely awake
until I began reciting the Lord's Prayer.
"Our father, who art in heaven..."
Your lips began to move
and slowly, softly, you spoke in concert with me
those ancient words, a part of you since you were a little girl.
Inseparable from your heart,
     your soul,
       your body,
         your Alzheimer's-ravaged brain.

"For thine is the kingdom"
You remembered those words when you could remember nothing else
spoken by the same Jesus who always remembers you
when you can remember nothing
other than the prayer he prayed

"And the power"
And even now, when your speech has been completely stilled
even now, when your blank stare blankly examines the ceiling
even now, when the staff at the care facility only have stories we can tell
of the piano
and the Air Force
and nursing school
and motherhood
to realize that you are one of the most
        precious
        and
        rare
human beings to ever walk the earth

"And the glory"
Even now, when your brain may have forgotten God

"Forever and ever"
God has not forgotten you.
"Forever and ever"
As you held your children, God holds you.
"Forever and ever"
As you loved your children, God loves you.
"Forever and ever"
And when you finally enter the home Jesus has prepared for you
"Forever and ever"
when you finish the race and meet the crowd of saints who have encouraged you
"Forever and ever"
I fully expect God to lovingly hold you, lovingly look in your eyes, and lovingly whisper to you:
"Forever and ever"
"Well done, good and faithful servant."
"Amen"

FORGIVENESS

"How can you be so stupid?"
I didn't think I was stupid.
But if an adult thought so
and not just any adult—a teacher
         my teacher
         my second-grade teacher
well, maybe I was wrong.
I was seven years old that school year.

"Why are you lying to me?"
Except I wasn't.
I knew it wasn't my arm
that brushed up against the Christmas tree
in the hallway
knocking a
shiny
red
glass
ball
ornament
to the floor where it
shattered
into
a million
shiny
blood red
pieces

as our class shuffled past
in what had been an orderly single-file line until
the horrible crash of breaking glass
pierced our eardrums and we all jumped
examining each other's faces for signs of guilt
wondering who was going to get in trouble.
"Why are you lying to me?"
I wasn't within a foot of that tree.
I knew it wasn't me and I said so
but the way she insisted that it had been
and that I was a horrible person for continuing to lie about it
well, maybe I was wrong.
I was seven years old that school year.

I no longer remember why I peed my pants
in the middle of class
just that I was sitting at my desk
My face growing red, as warm as
the growing dark spot
on my corduroys.
I remember choking back tears
as a puddle formed on my seat
dripping over the edges to the floor.
And I remember the way she looked at me—
it was not with compassion.
I was seven years old that school year.

Through second grade eyes,
                    adults are gods—
                    especially teachers.
Through second grade eyes,
adults are all-knowing and all-powerful—
                    especially teachers.

And so like an ancient priest
I spent the whole school year
when I was seven
attempting to discern how I had angered this god
who wielded such power
and discover the sacrifices I could offer
to appease her wrath.

Forty years later, I'm an adult.
I know adults aren't gods.
We are human.
We are fallible.
Sometimes, we are in pain.
Sometimes, we are broken.
Broken people tend to break people.

I was told as an adult
that no sacrifice I could have made
would have put back together
the shiny shards of the broken blood red glass ball
that was my second-grade teacher.
There had been a boy, her son,
who had died.
Sometimes, in her classes
she would discover
another boy,
a sacrificial lamb to offer
to her own god of grief
for propitiation of the sin
of her son's death.

Broken people tend to break people.
Often without trying.
Often without realizing.

I have tried seventy times seven times
to forgive.
I know I'm supposed to.
I know I want to.
I've even made the conscious decision
to forgive
but instead of forgiving and forgetting
my heart forgets that I've forgiven.

Am I proud that I sometimes
      Google her name
        to see if there's an obituary?
No. But I still look.

Do I think that her death (when it comes)
      will bring me life?
      Or healing?
      Or anything at all, really?
No. But I still look.

Sometimes when my inner depression voice
is doing its thing—
repeating
over
and
over
how worthless I am—
I wonder if she gave that voice
its vocal cords.

I was seven years old that school year.

Seven.

Forgive me, God.
I ought to forgive.
I want to forgive.
I need to forgive.
I'm just not there yet.

PSALM 22

My God, my God
what the fuck?
Why have you abandoned me
when everyone else has abandoned me too?
I expect people to let me down
even the ones I consider close
even family sometimes
but you? You?
I go about my day because I must
putting on a brave face
But inside? I'm falling apart
and at night, insomnia is a cruel bedmistress.

I've read the Bible and know the stories.
You healed the sick
brought back the dead
showed your face and rescued your people
time and time again when they needed you most.
Well I need you right now
and as far as I can see
you haven't done shit.

Everyone looks at me with scorn
or pity (which is actually worse).
They all assume I did something wrong
Or they tell me "This is all part of God's plan."

Bullshit.

Is this what you created me for?
Is this all that life means?
I swing between panic attacks
and the dark pit of depression.
Sometimes
I feel like It's just not worth it anymore.

And yet

I still haven't given up
dammit.
I still haven't given up
on me
And I guess since I'm talking to you
That means I haven't given up
on you either.

Don't get me wrong God
I meant all that stuff I said but
if I said it
there must be a part of me that realizes
you listen.

And if I'm being honest with myself
I guess I've seen your presence
with the poor
with the sick
with the dying
with the lost
with the lonely.

That's where you're active.
That's where you're doing your work.
That's where your humble glory shines
and that's right where I am
right now
My God my God

DUST

On a shelf in my bedroom closet sits a nondescript cardboard box
with a lid that I now keep closed
so that I don't rend the curtain
separating the present from the past
like I did once while searching for something unimportant.
Suddenly it was a different day
a Thursday in May
when my house was on fire
and I was crying.

I wasn't bothered so much by
the blackened corners of my son's birth certificate
      or the charred remains of my wife's to-do list
      or even my daughter's burnt report card
No.
It was the smoky ashen scent from inside.
Do you know that smell? Do you?
Like a fire pit the day after roasting marshmallows and singing songs
and laughing
like a fireplace hours after all the hot cocoa has been consumed
and the TV movie is over
and the family is upstairs dreaming sweet dreams.

Do you know that smell? Do you?
Because if you had been there on that particular Thursday
when my house was on fire
and I was crying

inside the box it would smell like death to you
like it does to me.

I have no need for the smell of death emanating from the ashes
so I keep that box closed
safely tucked away on the shelf
so I can't see the outside
nor smell the inside

And yet I know it's there.
I remember it exists
I recognize it remains
containing scorch-scented remains of the day.
It would be so simple
to toss that damn box away
removing the reminder
of when my house was on fire
and I was crying.

One Wednesday each year
the pastor at my church traces ashes—
a cross across my forehead—and pronounces

"remember that you are dust
and to dust you shall return."

Those ashes smell like olive oil and incense
                    they smell like holiness
                    they smell like tradition
(which says to burn palm leaves
The same ones saved from last year's
Holy Week hosannas)

They don't smell like my box.

Remember that your son's birth certificate is dust
                              (and so is he)
Remember that your wife's list is dust
                              (and so is she)
Remember that your daughter's report card is dust
                              (and so is she)
Remember that you are dust
and to dust you shall return.

Those boxed ashes don't smell pretty.
There's no oil and incense transforming them
into a pleasant traceable paste for forehead crosses.

These are my real ashes
that I keep closed off and hidden away.
Despite hearing the holy pastoral pronouncement
despite receiving the sacred sign
I have no need for the Ash Wednesday smell
of my house on fire.

And I was crying
remember that you are dust
And to dust you shall return.

SECTION 2: THE CROSS IN OUR NEIGHBOR

ARTISTRY

Dedicated to Alice and Jessica

In school I was taught
that in physics, black is the absence of light
and white contains all the colors
and I also learned about white history
                    from white textbooks
I read white literature
                    by white authors
I studied white leaders
                    taught by white teachers

There were black characters in white history
        (three-fifths as many as you'd expect)
and there were black characters in white books
        (always the foils, sometimes the servants, never the protagonists)
and there were exactly two black leaders
Harriet and Martin
        (whitewashed through white eyes)

But
I never took art
So I never learned that when it comes to paint
                  and pigment
                  (and melanin too)
white repels all the colors,
reflecting them back
but Black absorbs all the colors.

Black draws them in
Black holds them, embraces them.

Artist God, creator of color,
creator God, artist of eternity,
three in one, one in three,
the Holy Trinity's very essence
paints a portrait of divinely diverse unity
beyond comprehension or explanation.
She forms and he shapes humanity in their diverse image,
with a palette broad enough to hold all colors,
all sizes, all genders, all appearances.
With bold, broad, brush strokes she fills the canvas of the cosmos,
flinging joyful color throughout the world,
                across the galaxies,
                to the corners of the universe.
And when these hues all join in vibrant
                diverse
                unity
what our human eyes see is
        beautiful Blackness.
Despite what I was taught to know
Black contains the whole rainbow.

St. Francis (Not His Real Name)

I know a saint
you might have noticed him last week
      rummaging through the dumpster
      behind the Mexican grocery store on the corner
he told me afterward that he hadn't found much
although one time there was a lamp
(he was pretty sure it had been brass)
which would've looked nice in his apartment
but walking home he had seen a familiar face
who had just moved into an actual home after
      years
      on the streets
so he gave the lamp to him
      (after all, he already had one next to the
      mattress on the floor in the bedroom where he
      would read the Bible before bed)

Saint Francis (not his real name of course)
apologizes as he gets in my car
says he probably still smells like the dumpster
and I don't think he believes me when I say no he doesn't
(though he really doesn't)
but I offer him
      a squeeze from the hand sanitizer bottle
      and a mint
and he says he feels better

Saint Francis (not his real name)
rolls up his sleeves to show me his arms
old track marks trace maps of former drug-addled journeys
but nothing new today
I've told him before he really doesn't need to do that
but he always says
it makes him proud
I know there's plenty of other places a needle could pierce
     but
     I've seen him high
     and today he's not

Facial crevices deepen with his toothless smile
(crystal meth is an unforgiving demon)
as he asks about the apartment I'm taking him to
he had one before
     the one with the lamp and the mattress
     which are now probably in a dumpster
     somewhere
unless someone else rummaged
     and retrieved them

But things happen
(crystal meth is an unforgiving demon)
     he's no longer there
     and not yet somewhere else
not on the street (technically, at least at night)
but rummaging through dumpsters during the day
hiding from the unforgiving demon
     which torments him
     at the place he spends his nights
     these days

he says at least it's not the street (technically)
but there are times he wonders
      if the street would be better

St. Francis (not his real name) prays
for the guy sleeping in the dumpster he was rummaging through
last week
behind the Mexican grocery store
and for addicts
like the people who took him in
so he wouldn't be on the street (technically)
he says
      they shoot up every night
      creating their own track marks
      on their own arms
and it's killing him to watch them
he wants it so bad
      so bad it hurts
      so bad all he can do is pray
not for himself but them

St. Francis (not his real name) tells me
he prays for me too
not that I find him a place to live
(though he wants it so bad)
but that I'm happy
      healthy
          fulfilled

Little does he know
that through the very act of praying
his prayer is answered.

REQUIEM FOR A HERESY

"Hate the sin, love the sinner," he said sweetly,
with what I'm sure he thought was a friendly smile.
As if that settled it.
As if there was nothing left to say.
As if he hadn't just erased the created goodness
of God's beloved Tami
>>> or Mikah
>>> or Lauren
>>> or Bradley
>>> or Rosey
>>> or Archer
>>> or Jean
>>> or Abby
or even more whom I hold dear among all the millions of others,
most of whom I'll never know—
>> too many of whom live in the fear
>> of letting anyone know.
After all, when the (ironic air quotes) "sin" in question
is the sin of existing,
the sin of being who you are,
the sin of daring to love another person who loves you back
the sin of having the audacity to live as your God-given gender
then despite the theological contortions
>> and the linguistic somersaults
hating the sin means hating the sinner.

And hating the sinner?
A godly obligation.
Name calling,
       exclusion,
       discrimination,
       violence,
no longer themselves sins to hate,
but the carrying out of (ironic air quotes) "God's Will"
against that which God hates,
       those whom God hates,
       those whom God cannot accept,
       those for whom Jesus did not die.

When the sinner becomes the sin,
trite phrases transform into eternal death sentences
just as unjust as the one
executed two millennia ago
executing the One you claim to follow.
So, Mister Smiling "Hate the Sin, Love the Sinner
As If That Wraps It All Up Neatly in A Nice Little Christian Box?"
Jesus didn't die for that heresy. Fuck off.

FRED

Mr. Rogers used to appear on television
right after Sesame Street
he would amble into his television house

do the sweater and shoe thing
sing his song as I sang along
and call everyone neighbor

guests
strangers
diverse ethnicities

diverse occupations
people who looked and lived like me
people whose lives were

decidedly different from mine
he even asked if I would be his neighbor
(the answer was always yes)

one Sunday at church my young ears
perked up when the pastor preached on
the Good Samaritan

and being a neighbor
and helping others who may be different from you
I had heard the word neighbor so often every day

right after Sesame Street
the connection was immediate
which was the point and the genius

of the daily sermon Mr. Rogers lived

BEN

Concrete collapsing
metal beams and supports giving way
mountains of rubble standing where
you had just been standing in a
six-story building
before the earth shook.
Trapped
your body crushed
        broken
             dying
yet your voice is alive
not speaking
but singing
     O Lamb of God, you bear the sin
     of all the world away;
a song of reconciliation after pain
a song of new beginnings after the end
a song of new life after death
     Eternal peace with God you made:
     give us your peace, we pray.
your final words on earth
       the *Agnus Dei*
ancient words from ancient liturgy
     words made new
each time the church universal sings them
words stronger than steel supports and
         concrete walls

speaking of a promise stronger than death.

You sang your way through life
your life itself a song of justice for all
                              grace for all
                              peace for all
and even when that earthly life
                                        was
                                        slipping
                                        away
your final words
with your final breath
were a sung prayer for peace
as you sang your way to paradise.

GROUNDED

We are the stuff of the earth,
      fashioned from the dirt
           in a grand molecular tapestry.
Knit together with elemental sinews
connecting bone with bone,
      flesh with flesh,
           humanity with creation.
Pushed from the womb at birth
in a rush of blood and water
      sweat and tears
           pain and joy.

We are the stuff of the air,
with traces of Eden's lifebreath
lingering in our lungs
inhaling the ever-creating Divine Wind
Who breathed life into humanity.
Exhaling the ever-expanding Big Bang
which birthed the universe into being.

When the beat of our holy heart rhythm
                  is stilled
and we breathe our final breath,
we are drawn back to the stuff
from which we came.
           Re-entering the womb of the earth,
      born again to the ground,
as dust becomes dust once more.

SECTION 3: THE CROSS IN THE WORLD

On My Way to Church
Easter Morning

A garish patchwork quilt
of bumper stickers
assaulted my eyes at the red light

among the multicolored assortment
of nationalist politics, firearm idolatry,
and attacks on the fourth estate

a certain patch caught my eye
"Heaven Has a Wall
and Strict Immigration Policies"

a photo on my morning newsfeed
had also caught my eye earlier
during breakfast:

a multitude of shithole country
caged children
not yet robed in white

as their Great Tribulation continued
despite the promises
of a new administration.

I wondered what sort of hellish heaven
would have a wall
to deny entrance to these children

what sort of grotesque god
would malevolently mend the torn temple curtain
to hide the Holy One from these children

what sort of grotesque person
would pray for such a god's will to be done
on earth as it is in heaven

what sort of savior
would welcome the outcast
proclaim liberation for the oppressed

call his followers to a life
of love and service
and then by dying a grotesque death

shut out the huddled masses
of unbelieving undesirables
the shithole sinners yearning to breathe free

with a wall
to hold back
the wretched refuse

and policies
encoded in a book of books
enforcing their banishment.

The nation-healing leaves
on that Revelatory tree
have yet to spring forth

and the río de la vida
thirsting for water
from a still-dry spring

looks suspiciously like the Río Grande
though the water level is low
(it's been a dry spring).

The light turned green and
as the stickered sedan pulled away
one last slogan caught my eye--

unironically stuck in the center
and faintly faded it simply stated
"Jesus Saves."

O LITTLE TOWN

Watching the news when I was young
I remember the word

      Palestinian

spoken as a curse
synonymous with death and terror
hijackings and bombings.
Tom Brokaw
and Peter Jennings
and Dan Rather
the Holy Trinity of the 5:30 broadcast
broadcast the latest atrocities
committed by Palestinian terrorists.
Those two words—Palestinian terrorists—
became redundant synonyms in our national vocabulary.
There's something about a label
that dehumanizes
        the humans
           on the other side.

O little West Bank Palestinian town of Bethlehem
how still we see thee lie?
A giant wall, a barrier to the world
       a barrier to peace
       blocks our view.
We can't see thee lying or standing or resting or

playing or praying or working or hoping.
Sometimes walls are built to keep things out
and sometimes to keep things in—
separated and caged
untouchable and animal.
There's something about a wall
that dehumanizes
                    the humans
                        on the other side.
And it goes both ways.

O little besieged West Bank Palestinian town of Bethlehem
inhabited by Muslim Palestinians
and Christian Palestinians
whose shared identity is their walled dehumanization
in whose shared language both mosques and churches
pray to Allah.
Praying for peace
but not just peace—a just peace.

I once had dinner in a Palestinian home
with a Palestinian family
in the walled-in little besieged West Bank Palestinian town of Bethlehem.
They looked nothing like the images
Peter Jennings used to show me at 5:30.
Amid the crosses adorning the living room walls
I beheld laughter and teasing
                    prayer and love
                        prodigal hospitality
and mountains of food.
"Shukran," I said
(it was the one Arabic word I knew).
"Shukran, thank you, I can't possibly eat another bite."

There's something about a meal
that humanizes
                    the humans
                            on the other side of the table.
In the breaking of bread that night
communing in the holy communion of a meal
walls were torn down.
No longer caged in
no longer kept out
no longer Palestinian or American
no longer Jew or Greek
no longer slave or free
no longer male or female
for we were one in Christ Jesus.
Shukran, Allah.

IDOLATRY

Parchment promises shining sharply
     fancy letters scrawled in dried blood,
brown and peeling over the course of
more than two centuries
     require fresh flowing red ink
coursing
     from the veins of our children
     who ask for an egg but to whom we hand
     a venomous snake snapping with
     bullet-shaped fangs
spilling
     from the arteries of our enemies
     as we pray
     (for their deaths)
spurting
     from the still-beating hearts of our neighbor
     who we leave along the side of the road
     to Jericho

Our sulfur scented shiny shotgun idol
fashioned
     in the image of our rights
forged
     in the sweat of our freedom
hammered
     into shape with each shot
triggered
     by our fear
(despite our desperate protestations to the contrary)

demands
its violent sacrifice
and
weeping
we
offer
it.

We pray as we willingly hand over our children
We the People pray as we willingly hand over our neighbors
We the People of the United States of America pray that it is not us who
is handed over next.

The idolatrous ink runs red once more
and we wash our hands of the whole affair
trying in vain to keep the fresh blood from dripping
on our Sunday best
while consoling ourselves

because after all
what more could we possibly do?

THE SECOND COMMANDMENT

Grownups always said
not to take the Lord's name in vain
so "Oh my God" was taboo
and while "damn it" was frowned upon
"God damn it" was absolutely off limits.

I was careful with my language--
though I broke two commandments at once
when I coveted and subsequently stole
Robby's SR-71 Hot Wheels plane
and had no interest in keeping the sabbath
(except for the cute girl in Sunday School)
and mostly honored my father and mother to their faces
but constantly broke that one
under my breath
behind their backs
when I was mad.

But the Lord's name? Simple.
Just don't mention God if you curse.
Right?

Years later I watched planes fly into the World Trade Center.
Gripped by
        shock
        numbness
        fear

anger
all I could say was
"Oh my God."
It was the only prayer I had.
"Oh my God. Oh my God. Oh. My. God."
A cry for comfort.
A plea for peace.
All other words perished in the explosions.

Another day a man with a gun strolled into
an elementary school in Connecticut.
Minutes later, twenty young children
lay in their own blood, brutally murdered.

The terror these children faced,
and their teachers—
some who gave their bodies and lives as human shields...
three words escaped my mouth through clenched teeth:
"God damn it."
This too—yes, a prayer.
God, damn this violence
to the hell that it represents.
God, damn the personal sin
and the systemic sin
that lead to tragedies like this.
Damn the evil, God.
Curse it.
Banish it from the earth.
God damn it.

On TV I sometimes see preachers
with pearly white teeth

to match the pearly white Rolls Royces
they keep in their pearly white mansions
that they bought in God's name
with the money
given by their congregations in God's name
and speaking gigs in God's name
and book deals in God's name
(they look nothing like the preachers I know).

And I see spineless politicians wildly waving
unread Bibles with unharmed spines
simply to court a voting segment
for the next election.

And I see God's name used to
       discriminate against women
          discriminate against the LGBTQ+ community
       discriminate against other religions.

I think differently now than I did as a child
about what it means
to take the Lord's name in vain.

REPENT

I repent.
I repent of feeling unworthy—
 unworthy of love,
 unworthy of good things,
 unworthy of respect
 (even self-respect).
I repent.

I repent.
I repent of not speaking my truth
when speaking would make me (or someone else)
uncomfortable,
valuing my comfort over doing what is right,
wanting to smooth things over,
running my hands over the surface of an unconsummated conflict
like smoothing out an uncomfortable comforter
which is crushing me,
smiling (though secretly gasping for air).
Why do I smile as the weight of my lies
 slowly asphyxiates my soul,
      my will?
I repent.

I repent.
I repent of the times
I've been unaware of my privilege—
   my white privilege,

my male privilege,
my straight privilege,
my cisgender privilege,
my Christian privilege—
when I've taken for granted that doors open to me
are closed to others,
that I am invited to tables
where others may not sit,
that I am allowed and even encouraged to speak
when the voices of others are silenced,
that I am endowed with certain inalienable rights.

Life—
when my black neighbors disproportionately die,
when a traffic stop
or a hoodie
or holding a cell phone
or even being asleep in your own apartment
can and does lead to death.
I repent.

Liberty—
when my queer neighbors can't marry who they love,
can't hold hands while taking a walk,
can't even use the fucking bathroom which fits their gender,
can't live or work or shop in places where I can because the law says
people like me can discriminate against them,
just because we feel like it.
I repent.

The pursuit of happiness—
when my undocumented neighbors
are pursued by ICE,

my female neighbors
              are pursued by a culture of rape,
my Muslim neighbors
              are pursued by religious bigotry.
I repent.

Create in me a clean heart O God
and renew a right spirit within me:
a spirit emboldened to speak,
a spirit empowered to serve,
a spirit of repentance.
I repent.

WHITE AMERICAN JESUS

White American Jesus walks with me
and he talks with me in the public
garden downtown on my lunch break and he

tells me he is my own—wait, the hymn
says the opposite—did he mean to say that?
White American Jesus chuckles

and brushes a fly from his face—
he didn't misspeak, he says. An office
building just east of the garden still burned out from

last summer's protests casts strange shadows
surrounding us. A black man died in Minneapolis
while resisting arrest (fairly sure I heard

he had drugs in his system) so radicals
honored a dead criminal by blocking traffic
and destroying property. I shake my head sadly

at the loss of respect for law and order
amid meaningless discrimination accusations
sowing seeds of divisiveness

perpetually blaming white privilege for their own
perpetual problems while
perpetually burning buildings and attacking police

setting their blame at the foot
of a burning white cross
is the real racism.

Privilege? One thing I've never possessed is
privilege. Work, morals, love for God and
love for country—that's how I'm here

and not through any sort of fake privilege.
Their divisiveness is what's
tearing us apart

instead of bringing us together in the
unity they want.
A clanging cymbal crashes through

my reverie rant with the opening bars of
a ditty by Duke as a local group launches into
their Jazz in the Park lunch set.

White American Jesus must have been reading
my mind as he loudly proclaims to me
his voice a noisy gong to be heard above the

instrumental cacophony
"You have heard it said black lives matter, but I say to you
Blue Lives Matter—

yea, All Lives Matter"
(just as I had suspected).
He reassures me that

I don't have a racist bone in my body.
I have black friends and
have never (not even once) used the N-word.

A tree set in the center attracts our
attention with a bold lettered sign I hadn't
seen on previous walks with White American Jesus.

TREES TREATED FOR PESTS
PICKING FRUIT HARMFUL
AND PUNISHABLE BY EXPULSION

White American Jesus mutters something
about rendering to Caesar while plucking an apple
polishing it on his robe and offering it to me.

God created fruit to be eaten
you look famished
take and eat
biting through the skin
juice running down my chin
soft sweet flesh of
strange fruit
strangely refreshing
I recognize I hadn't eaten all day.

Nearby sits the homeless man begging
as he does daily with his misspelled cardboard sign
so I slip him a crumpled dollar.

White American Jesus nods in approval.
"God bless you," the bum tells me
(wait—did the PC Police outlaw "bum?")

and I smile because indeed I have been
#blessed for my faithfulness and hard work.
It feels good to give back and pay it forward

like I did yesterday when I paid the bill for the guy
in the Lexus behind me in the Starbucks drive thru
but this panhandler

I've prayed for him
to better his life
yet here he still sits.

"God helps those who help themselves,"
White American Jesus sagely says
and I nod in approval of his wisdom.

I've heard that proverb often in Bible studies
though I can't remember chapter or verse
off the top of my head.

"If he just grabs hold of his bootstraps and tries
to pull himself up I will reward his efforts,"
White American Jesus patiently explains

"but he'd rather mooch money than
earn it so giving him only a dollar #blesses him
infinitely more than free food or housing

or healthcare from Caesar would"
echoing the words of the godly politician I voted for
in the last election.

White American Jesus affirms my ideas:
handouts harm
enabling disability and impairing incentive.

He has not #blessed the fruits of my labors
only to have them snatched up
and misused by Caesar so

there's not much White American Jesus can do
for this guy. But as it's written
he won't give him any more than he can handle.

White American Jesus seems to be attracting
more flies now buzzing around his milky
white face as he tells me how thankful he is

that there are still followers
like me who perceive the spiritual warfare
struggling for the soul of this godly nation

and who are done with daily
perverse
pervasive
persecution
by his
eternal enemy—

—and suddenly the sky is swirling I am falling and eaten apple
core more flies growing flying flies flocking flitting fluttering gutter
gutting White race American mine mine buzzing personal Jesus flashing
flies floating eyes serpents wilderness temptation temple hunger
horsemen bowels beast Beelzebub
anti
anti
anti

Christ.
Lunch is over but He is always with me.
I'll walk with White American Jesus again tomorrow.

SLEEP IN HEAVENLY PEACE

They say there is a war on Christmas
and I believe them.
I have seen battle lines drawn
I have heard sergeants shouting orders
to the fraudulently faithful
goose stepping toward Bethlehem.
"Tell me where he is so that I too may worship him."

There's a nativity scene on my table
crafted from olive wood
by a Palestinian artisan
from a Palestinian town.
The figures are faceless
but I imagine Mary with steel eyes
memorizing her son's every divine detail.
As the marching draws nearer
she shields him from the garish lights
she covers his ears so that the constant ringing
of millions of cash registers
doesn't awaken him.
Leaning in I listen
as she softly sings
a magnificent Magnificat lilting lullaby
the tune echoing the wind
that hovered over the primordial water
in the beginning
a stirring of memory in her slumbering son
recreating creation.

She softly sings the real reason
for the season:
the hungry hungering no more
(Silent night)
the last and lost becoming the first and found
(Holy night)
the cast of outcasts no longer cast out
(All is calm)
power
turned
upside
down.

All is bright as the battle nears mother and child.

Suddenly
the holy infant
God-With-Us, God-For-Us
is ripped from his mother's grasp.
Screaming she struggles to save her son
from friendly fire machine gun aural ammunition
scourging his tender and mild skin.

TheyaretakingtheChristoutofChristmasandthesestores
onlysayhappyholidayssowewillnotshopthereanymoreand
whyisntherenoChristmastreeinthetownsquareobviously
theworldhatesChristiansbecauselookathowweareoppressed
andsuppressedeventhoughwehaveaplaceofpowerinsociety
andhelpingthepoortakesawayincentivetoworkiftheyarehungry
theyneedtoworkmore

With thirty pieces of self-righteousness
those who claim to follow his name
betray the Bethlehem baby
carrying him away
goose stepping toward Golgotha.

One more victim
in the Slaughter of the Innocents
crucified on a cross of tinsel
pierced by dogmatic nails
persecuting while claiming to be persecuted
wielding power while claiming to be powerless
opposing and killing The Reason for the Season
while insisting that others remember it.

A sign hangs above the child's head:
"This is the King of the Persecuted Powerful."
And a sword pierces Mary's heart too.

My God, my God, why have we forsaken him?

SNOW SEX

I.
Apparently the Inuits are incredibly specific
when it comes to snow, which doesn't surprise me
I suppose, with the amount of it they see.

Nebraska winters can be mildly snowy, but we
don't have fifty or a hundred terms for snow
(or whatever the actual number is) like the Inuits.

One could create English words to differentiate
between the big flakes that fall
when it's just below freezing,

which upon hitting the ground become heavy
and clumpy and can cause heart attacks
when out of shape retired men try to shovel,

but which kids (too young to worry about things like
widow-makers and shoveling) love because it's perfect
for snowmen and snowball fights from behind snow forts;

and the light, powdery stuff looking so much
like salt, I've sometimes imagined scooping some up
with a gloved hand, bringing it inside

and seasoning the comfort food
that's been simmering in the slow cooker
since before the snow even started in the morning.

Sometimes, this snow is merciful
and doesn't require a shovel—
a gas-powered leaf blower does the trick.

Even grouchy adults can find joy
painting airbrushed designs
in the frosty tabula rosa of their driveway.

I don't build snowmen or snow forts anymore
but I do shovel, so that grainy sort of snow is my favorite
(even though my kids find it to be a complete waste of moisture).

II.
There's probably a rule
in some composition textbook somewhere
that a poem shouldn't be self-referential

but this poet just took seven and a half stanzas
to describe two types of snow
when the Inuits could have done it in two words

and all their Inuit friends would have immediately
nodded their heads knowingly,
simultaneously remembering

dear Uncle Alfred who had a heart attack while shoveling
the one kind and hoping whatever snow came next
would be the other kind.

The more intimately we know a thing,
the more a part of our life and culture it is,
the more necessary it becomes

to describe it in shorthand
so we don't spend seven conversational stanzas
describing something that could take two words.

III.
A Christian once told me their Bible was
a word-for-word translation
from the original languages and I wondered

how an Inuit Bible translation would render
malakoi and *arsenokoitai*
with one word each when they describe

something as complex as Inuit snow
because 1611 King James English
with nuanced human sexuality vocabulary

obviously got it exactly right with just one word
and we should all be forever thankful
that 17th century British Puritanism

with its intimate knowledge and
accepted acculturation of ancient
Roman sexual practices

discovered the one accurate
Alpha and Omega word for us
so we in the 21st century could

finally understand
the will of God
now and forever amen.

SECTION 4: THE CROSS IN THE CHURCH

AVE MARIA

He was cradled in her womb
a mass of cells fueled by a divine spark
growing
developing
moving
listening
when his mother sang a revelation—
a song of divine revolution

Bringing down the powerful and lifting the lowly
(the last will be first and the first will be last)
filling the hungry
(blessed are those who hunger for they shall be filled)
and sending away the rich
(camels travel through needles more easily than the rich enter heaven)
a song of divine mercy
(blessed are the merciful)
and fulfilled divine promises
(I came not to abolish the law but to fulfill it)

The babe who suckled at the breast
of this bearer of God
and this singer of justice
he who played on her lap
who listened to her lessons
who increased in wisdom and in years
under her roof
is it any coincidence his words echoed hers?

At his homecoming
the son of the woman
who with full-throated joy sang the Magnificat
this boy who had begun to make a name for himself
when he showed up at the Nazareth synagogue
      are we really surprised
      when he selects the Isaiah scroll?
Are we really taken aback by the words he reads
      of bringing good news to the poor
      release to the captives
      sight to the blind
      setting the oppressed free
      and proclaiming jubilee?

He may have prayed
to the one he called Father
but I'm pretty sure Jesus was a mama's boy.

BELIEVABLE IMPERFECTION

I find Easter easier to believe than Christmas.
Not so much in the happened-ness
but in the telling.
Christmas reads like a wrapped box
packaged, tidy, beneath the tree.
The precious gift inside carefully considered,
the presentation perfect.
Isn't it, though? The scene set so well,
the well-ordered genealogical generations,
the census sweeping the Holy Family
out from their Nazareth home,
neatly depositing them in the City of David.
Angel choirs serenading shepherds
while magi bringing symbolic gifts
follow a star shining just for the event.
Even Herod's jealous infanticide (enter Pharaoh),
finding safety in Egypt (enter Bitiah),
and Promised Land return
leading people to salvation (enter Moses),
too perfect?
too calculated?
too...theologized?
No matter the details,
it's still the story
of God's love for humanity,
of God's taking on flesh,
of the inbreaking of God's reign

but
Easter. Ah, Easter.
A defeated band of once-devoted disciples
still staggering, their leader lost,
another criminalized victim crucified
by the violent Roman Peace.
And that third morning.
Confusion—where is the body?
Worry—was it stolen? Desecrated?
          slow realization
          breathless astonishment
          incredulous wonderment
no neatly fitting pieces or angel choirs
no making sense of what it means
no added theologizing
but rather running
announcing
disbelieving
questioning
and the aftermath?
Not boldly stepping out announcing to the world—
they and their proclamation still hide away
unsure of what to do
still living as though
Easter
      hasn't
         happened.
The believability is in the imperfection.
Imperfect people, responding imperfectly
with missteps
uncertainty
and an imperfectly faithful faith

to God's activity in the world.
Would we expect anything different?
Would I respond any differently?
Life doesn't arise out of an execution.
Victory doesn't arise out of humiliation.
Reconciliation doesn't arise out of sin.
Except through the cross.

WE WAIT EXPECTANTLY

An Advent Hymn
Tune: TERRA PATRIS ("This is My Father's World")

As the prophets had foretold
To a people bound in fear
In exile long out in Babylon
"God's kingdom soon will be near."
They wait expectantly
For the coming of the King
Who reigns alone over David's throne
And sets his people free.

As the angel had foretold
To a young, unmarried girl
"O chosen one, you will have a son,
Your baby will change the world."
She waits expectantly
For the coming of her boy
The child she'll bear is the God who cares
And fills the lowly with joy.

As the scriptures have foretold
So we live with hope each day
God's kingdom come, God's will be done
God's love has final say.
We wait expectantly
For the coming of the Lord
Who breaks the bonds of our sin so strong
Who shatters spear and sword.

In this Advent now we wait
But we hope for what could be.
God's mission here calls us far and near
To spread God's love and peace.
We wait expectantly
In a world that's filled with pain
Through our dark night, waiting for the light
The coming of God's final reign.

BLASPHEMOUS HOSANNAS

Hosanna (save us) is not
      a cry of (save us) praise
      a (save us) shout of thanksgiving
      a singsong synonym
      for alleluia (save us).

It isn't a fancy, frilly, churchy word
that we save all year to trot out
like a donkey
in fancy, frilly font
because the master has need of it.

No, hosanna is
      a plea (save us)
      an expectation (Save Us)
      a demand (SAVE US).

It is a threat.
Save us. Or else.

Save us from violence (with violence).
Save us from oppression (by oppressing).
Save us from the other (by excluding).

But don't you dare suggest
that all this fancy, frilly, churchy talk about
      love and

      forgiveness and
      peace
might require
      risk and
      vulnerability and
      pain.

No, don't you dare mess with our
hosanna expectations.

We will fucking crucify you for that blasphemy.

PROCESSION

Look here, this man holding a palm branch:
did you notice the slight limp
as he joined the crowd?
Jesus had fully healed him
when his friends lowered him through the roof...
but muscle memory is a funny thing.
He still forgets sometimes.

And this woman, the sun reflecting the oil still in her long hair:
those around her shout "Hosanna!" "Save us!"
Yet she speaks only through flowing tears,
as they flowed that day when she washed his feet.
He has already saved her.

Over there, a man near the back holds his daughter up on his shoulders
so she can see the one
who brought her back to life.

And this, this is a sight.
A group of seven, eight, no, nine
nine men adorned with rags and palm branches
waving and calling out, "thank you!"
"Thank you!"
Jostled and bumped by the growing crowd,
former leprous untouchables not quite used to the feeling
of being touched
or of even standing in the midst
of healthy people.

These two women next to each other,
what is the one on the left writing in the dirt
as she crouches down,
and why does she smile as she hears him
proclaim that the very stones would cry out
if the people were silenced?
And her companion, is she Samaritan?
notice the knowing, reminiscent look as she brings
a handful of water to her lips on this hot day
and murmurs a quiet prayer in memory
of the four husbands she's buried.

We cast out, God gathers in.
We despise, God loves.
We draw lines, God erases.
Hosanna in the highest.

CHRISTUS VICTOR

If his death was the point,
        then what of the empty tomb?
If he was only a martyr in our place,
a propitiatory sacrifice
taking the brunt of God's wrath,
        then why Easter?
Was that morning in the garden a divine parlor trick?
Was the resurrection simply a theological necessity
to preserve the Trinity?
Was it the balancing of some sort of math equation
where to solve for x,
if x equals eternal life,
then God's grace and God's justice must cancel each other out?

There's no victory in parlor tricks.
There's no celebration in theological necessities.
There's no joy in balancing the scales of justice,
God still demanding a pound of flesh
but in an act of perichoretic self-mutilation,
taking it from Jesus's
hands
feet
side
life
instead of our own.

The work of the Christ did not culminate
                              on Good Friday.
It can be no other way,
or else we are of all people most to be pitied.

Give me an innocent Jesus
unjustly executed by the unholy union
of religious authority and political power,
anxious to eliminate the threat
of the justly subversive Reign of God
in its midst.

The power of exclusion
the power of oppression
the power of violence
the power of sin
the power of death itself—
when all the powers that oppose God
thought they had defeated this
Holy Troublemaker,
when they permanently set the stone to seal the prison door,
ready to declare victory,
and claim humankind as their prisoners
for eternity

God's wrath burned hot.

Not against the prisoners
          but against the jailers.
Not against sinners
          but against the power of sin.
Mama bear God leapt into battle—

snarling, slashing,
stopping at nothing to protect and free her children.
Bringing life out of death, Jesus rolled the stone away
and imprisoned humankind emerged unfettered,
knowing forevermore that no matter what may come
the power of God, the power of grace
reigns supreme.

So give me Easter as a ticker tape parade
celebrating the liberation of a people.
Give me the united song of all creation
singing with wild abandon.
Give me dancing in the streets,
orchid corsages and lilies bursting with color,
fancy hats kept in boxes and reserved for special occasions
flung into the air like graduation caps
on the day of commencement.
For this is the commencement of the feast that will have no end,
the feast of victory for our God.
Christ is risen!
Christ is risen indeed!
Alleluia!

EMMAUS

A pregnant moment
laboring in the seeing
crying out in the hearing
the crowning finally comes
in the breaking
of the bread
and the burning heart births an epiphany
the answer was
right there
walking with you on the road
the answer is right here
in the Bread
      broken for you
with the Bread
      given to you
under the Bread
      consumed by you

Bread of Life
always with you
(even to the end of the age)

BUT I SAY TO YOU

Let anyone who has ears to hear, listen!
It has been said
all his friends abandoned him
all his followers were nowhere to be found
all his disciples were paralyzed with fear
but I say to you:
look for the women.

Go ahead, do it.
Read of the arrest
       the crucifixion
       the resurrection.
Read from all four gospels.
Read their names.
Look for the women.

Who was at the cross?
Who came out of hiding to care for the body?
Who discovered the empty tomb?
Who was the first evangelist of the risen Christ?
Look for the women.

Were it not for the courage of the women
the steadfastness of the women
the presence of the women
the voices of the women
the faith of the women

the
church
would
not
exist.

So
why are the spiritual descendants
of the first ones to proclaim the resurrection
unwelcome in the church's pulpits?
Who has stilled their voices
dismissing them as tellers
of idle tales?
When it was the women who led the way
through the pain and confusion of
Good Friday
Holy Saturday
Easter Sunday
why is their leadership invalidated
in the sometimes painful and often confusing present?

Who disempowers the ones Jesus empowered?
Who devalues the ministry of the ones Jesus valued?
Who patronizes the patrons of Jesus's ministry?
For two thousand years
        who has intentionally
        and systematically
        erased these women of faith
from the collective Christian consciousness
and rejected their divine calling?

Let anyone who has ears to hear, listen!
You have heard it said:
>   in the Bible
>   look for the men
>   in proclamation
>   listen to the men
>   in leadership
>   obey the men
But I say to you:
smash the fucking patriarchy.

LORD WE WAIT FOR YOU IN DARKNESS

An Advent Hymn
Tune: BEACH SPRING (Lord Whose Love in Humble Service)

Lord we wait for you in darkness,
We await your promised light
As we wander through the wilderness
Still we live in deepest night
Do not turn your face forever
Hear our cry, "How long O Lord?"
Send a Savior, our messiah,
To forgive, redeem, restore.

God you promised through the prophets
You would set the pris'ners free.
Yet we're captive to our sinfulness
Bound by chains of suffering.
In an exile of our making
Still we lift our eyes to you
Please deliver us from evil
And your covenant renew.

The oppressed cry out for freedom
And the refugee for home
Different races and identities
Face rejection, walk alone
Rend the heavens, tear them open,

Bring your justice now to earth
As you've promised to be with us
We await our Savior's birth.

As your chosen people Israel
Waited for the promised one
So we too wait for the coming
Incarnation of your Son.
Not in Bethlehem alone, but
In our lives, and finally
On the day of truth and judgment
At the end of history.

SCAPEGOAT

Forget the portraits of bloodthirsty crowds,
of a scheming Sanhedrin,
of a race or a religion turning on one of its own.
Watching Holy Week through that distorted funhouse window mirror
twists the Star of David,
reshaping its lines and angles
into a swastika,
with Auschwitz its sacrificial temple,
burnt offerings in a deathly silent flurry
of floating fleshy ash
gently covering us in our shame.

No.
It is we who decide that it is better for one man
to die
than for us to relinquish our kingdoms,
our power,
our glory,
forever and ever.

The humble power of the servant God
threatens the safe certainty
of our self-fashioned self-righteous golden calf
(first commandment be damned).
Our betrayal comes in the garden with a kiss.

By our own power
and for our own power
we pound those Golgotha nails.
Not a race nor a religion nor a people
but our own grasping ambition clutching the hammer,
our craving for control scourging the savior,
our crown fashioned of self-righteous thorns
piercing his brow.

Forgive us, for we know exactly what we do.

GENESIS IS NOT A SCIENCE TEXTBOOK SO PLEASE STOP TREATING IT AS ONE

chaos
in the beginning
a flash of creative light energy
expanding across the cosmos
let there be
     and there was
         and it was good
breath of God hovering
voice of God creating
bringing order
     goodness
     life out of the
chaos
in gorgeously liturgical poetic prose

creation
the garden
the temptation
the fall
sibling rivalry
murder
human descent into
chaos

wiping the slate clean
cleansing creation through water
beginning anew
a promise of life through light
color
beauty
rainbow

the (genesis) beginning
rich
beautiful
meaningful
the story of God
the story of humanity
the story of a relationship
but only if we allow it to be what it is
only when we listen for the creative voice of God
speaking order
goodness
life
into our own
chaos

ACKNOWLEDGMENTS

My third-grade teacher, Ms. Kitty Fisher (previously Owen), who helped me put the pieces back together after a traumatic second grade year and encouraged me to write. You took me to the Young Authors conference in Marquette, and when asked that day by the local TV station if I wanted to be an author, I replied, "yes, certainly." I consider this book a promise fulfilled. Rest in peace, Ms. Owen.

Rev. Ron Youngerman, who confirmed me, helped shape my faith as a teenager, and whose encouraging influence on me continues yet today.

Rev. Larry Meyer, who had a gift for bringing out the gifts in others. Without your prodding I likely would never have made it to seminary. Thank you for your guidance in my young adult years, and thank you to your family, especially the Meyer sibs, for their sacrifices as you lived out your vocation.

Luther Seminary Distributed Learning Cohort 3. You are some of the most caring and faithful servants of God I know, and each of you has made an impact on my faith and in my life. You make the church better through your presence and leadership. Electric Leprechaun Boogie Woogie forever.

The faculty at Luther Seminary who taught me, challenged me, helped me discover my approach to theology, and showed me grace through one of the most difficult periods of my life.

Each of the names in *Requiem for a Heresy* is the actual first name of a living, breathing, child of God whom I personally know and love. My thanks to Tami, Mikah, Lauren, Bradley, Rosey, Archer, Jean, and Abby for their permission to include their names in that piece.

Those who served as my *de facto* proofreaders and editors: Adam Thayer, Kristen Paige, and Rev. Scott Johnson. Thank you for not running away screaming when I asked you to read "a book of Christian poetry." (And Scott, thank you for allowing me to borrow the brain while I was writing.)

All the countless other people who have loved, supported, and encouraged me along the way. I'd try to list you all, but as the Gospel of John says, "if every one of them were written down, I suppose that the world itself could not contain the books that would be written."